A VOICE for the SPIRIT Bears

"If together we can succeed in saving the spirit bear, we will have proved that one young person with no remarkable skills or intellect, but armed simply with a passion, can take hold of a cause and unite the world. After all, we are the voices for the sick, the poor, the children, the dreamers ... and the bears."

— *Simon Jackson*

For Doug, who walks beside me over jagged rocks and down slippery slopes and reminds me I can. And for Simon and Carol Ann — without your voices, there would be no story to tell. — C.O.

For Jay and Maggie. For Everything. — K.D.

Acknowledgments

When you work on a project for more than ten years, there are a lot of people to thank. I couldn't have made it this far in life without the unfailing love and support of my parents, who first planted the seed "You can do anything you set your mind to." To the villagers Donna Janell Bowman, Cynthia Leitich Smith, Debbie Gonzales, Anne Bustard, Sarah Aronson and Don Tate — thank you. This story went through numerous versions, and your support was instrumental in its delivery. To Barbara Kerley, Kim Griswell and the Highlights Foundation team, thank you for the nonfiction workshop that inspired me to never give up. To Bethany Hegedus, your encouragement and words of wisdom empowered me to see this story through Simon's eyes and to get to the emotional core. Stacey Roderick — we did it! Thank you for the many edits and questions that harnessed my ten-year-old voice and silenced the adult one. To my amazing literary agent, friend and mother hen Erzsi Deàk for all your support and for seeing the potential in this manuscript. I'll be forever grateful. To the Kids Can Press team, words cannot express my gratitude in helping this story see the light of day — the planet needs more heroes like David Simon Jackson. For Simon and Carol Ann, thank you for the many email exchanges, the phone conversations, the photographs and your time that allowed me to tell Simon's story in a way that will inspire new generations to use their voices and make a difference in the wild world. Many people have asked me why I didn't give up on this book, and the answer is quite simple — because Simon never gave up on the bears. And last, but far from least, to Doug, Cassidy, Halle and Wyatt — you are my beating heart, my life.

Kids Can Press gratefully acknowledges the financial support of the Government of Ontario, through the Ontario Media Development Corporation; the Ontario Arts Council; the Canada Council for the Arts; and the Government of Canada for our publishing activity.

Published in Canada and the U.S. by Kids Can Press Ltd.
25 Dockside Drive, Toronto, ON M5A 0B5

Kids Can Press is a Corus Entertainment Inc. company

www.kidscanpress.com

The artwork in this book is rendered with brush and ink, brushpen and pencil on paper, and colored digitally.

The text is set in ITC Goudy Sans Std.

Edited by Stacey Roderick and Katie Scott
Designed by Marie Bartholomew

Printed and bound in Shenzhen, China, in 10/2018 by C & C Offset

CM 19 0 9 8 7 6 5 4 3 2 1

Library and Archives Canada Cataloguing in Publication

Oliver, Carmen, author
    A voice for the spirit bears : how one boy inspired millions to save a rare animal / Carmen Oliver ; illustrated by Katy Dockrill.

ISBN 978-1-77138-979-2 (hardcover)

    1. Kermode bear — British Columbia — Great Bear Rainforest — Juvenile literature. 2. Jackson, Simon, 1982– — Juvenile literature. 3. Great Bear Rainforest (B.C.) — Juvenile literature. 4. Rain forest ecology — British Columbia — Juvenile literature. I. Dockrill, Katy, illustrator II. Title.

QL737.C27O37 2019   j599.78'5097111   C2018-902057-1

A VOICE for the SPIRIT Bears

How One Boy Inspired Millions to Save a Rare Animal

Carmen Oliver • Katy Dockrill

CitizenKid™

A collection of books that inform children about the world and inspire them to be better global citizens

Kids Can Press

Simon peered through a telescope from a
lookout post in Yellowstone National Park.
Hours ticked by. Rain soaked his clothes.
    Still, he didn't budge.

Finally, a mother grizzly bear emerged
from the pine forest with two playful cubs
by her side. She was huge, especially when
she stood on her hind legs. Coyotes quickly
retreated. No one messed with a grizzly.
    Seven-year-old Simon wished *he* was
as powerful as a bear.

Back home, he felt anything but powerful. Words formed clearly
in his head, but when he opened his mouth, the sounds collided.
It's just nervousness that makes him stutter, the doctor said
reassuringly. *He'll be fine*.

On the playground, Simon didn't feel fine. Kids teased him,
chose him last or not at all.

But in the woodlands behind his house, he felt happier. There
he talked easily to the squirrels. He photographed the wildlife.
He read and reread books, especially his favorite one about a
grizzly named Wab.

Simon also liked watching the news with his parents. One day, there was a story about a forest above Canada's border in Alaska that needed protection. The trees were going to be cut down, destroying the homes of the brown bears that lived there.

Those bears are helpless, thought Simon. *It's not fair!*

The next day, he opened a lemonade stand. "H-h-help save the bears," he called as people passed by. He wrote to the Canadian prime minister and the president of the United States and sent the sixty dollars he'd raised to stop the cutting.

Simon was thrilled when a few months later he heard on the news that a park had been created for the bears. His words had helped make a difference!

LEMONADE

HELP
save
THE
BEARS

In school, it was harder to make a difference. Instead of
waiting for Simon to get his words out, kids finished his
sentences for him. Most lunchtimes, he ate in the bathroom
to avoid bullies. On those tough days, Simon focused on
his love of bears, reading about them for hours.

The summer he turned thirteen, he became fascinated
by a rare type of black bear called the spirit bear. One
in ten of these special bears was born with the creamy
white fur that gave them their name. And they were
found only in the Great Bear Rainforest. That
was just a few hours' journey from his home!

But there, too, loggers were shrinking the
bears' habitat by cutting down trees. Once again,
Simon felt he had to do something. But what?

If one letter had worked before, he thought,
imagine what lots *of letters could do.*

As Simon stood in front of his classmates, his legs shook. His hands were sweaty. His brain raced. *Be powerful, like the grizzly from Yellowstone,* he told himself. *TRY.* The spirit bears had no voice, so he had to find his. He opened his mouth and ...

... his words spilled out and snapped into place!

"By protecting the home of the spirit bears, we can ensure that they will be wild and free forever." Simon went on to explain that if the bears were chased from their home to live among regular black bears, these rare animals would be lost forever.

He visited every classroom in the school. He convinced students to put pen to paper. To stand up for what was right.

Seven hundred letters flooded the government.

But the cutting continued.

Simon refused to give up. "Talking to people is like dropping a pebble in the pond and seeing the ripples," he told his mom. "If I reach one person, they can reach another, and so on."

So he wrote out what he needed to say. He memorized the words and rehearsed, again and again — a trick he had discovered that stilled his stuttering.

Wanting to be taken seriously, he visited businesses and other schools wearing his suit and tie. Some of the kids made fun of him, calling him "Bear Boy" and "weirdo" — words that stung.

Stand tall, like the grizzly from Yellowstone, Simon kept reminding himself.

The next year, Simon asked some friends to help him start a group they would call the Spirit Bear Youth Coalition. His idea was that students from around the world — kids who cared about the bears the way he did — could share information in school and online.

In time, millions joined, boosting his confidence.
Simon even found himself writing to journalists
and thundering away at rallies for the environment.
"By saving the spirit bears, you're protecting
all the other life around them!"

More and more people began to pay attention. Famous actors, pop stars and members of royalty joined their voices with Simon's. He even became friends with the world-famous wildlife conservationist Dr. Jane Goodall, who had become interested in Simon's work after meeting him on a boat trip.

Then a team of researchers asked Simon
to join their expedition to study spirit bears.
It was the chance of a lifetime.

He begged his parents to let him go,
even though actually seeing one of
the white bears would be a long shot.
Finally, they said yes.

YES!

For days, Simon and the team hiked over
jagged rocks, across streams and down
slippery slopes in the Great Bear Rainforest.
To Simon, it felt like they were walking in a
forest right out of a fairy tale.

Then one afternoon, as he crouched
in a bed of leafy skunk cabbage, Simon
heard a twig snap. He looked up and saw a
chocolate-eyed spirit bear sniffing the air.

"Stay still," one of the researchers
whispered. "We don't want him to feel
threatened in any way."

Simon stayed calm, and his words to the
bear came easily: "I won't let you down."

With that, the spirit bear ambled
away, taking Simon's promise with it.

And Simon did keep his promise.

For the next few years, he continued to work with other activists, forestry companies, local Indigenous communities and the government until, finally, land in the Great Bear Rainforest was awarded to the spirit bears.

Simon Jackson had given the spirit bears a voice, by first finding his own.

The Real Simon Jackson

A Voice for the Spirit Bears is based on the real life of David Simon Jackson, whose lifelong work as a protector of the environment began at an early age.

Simon was born in 1982 and grew up in Vancouver, British Columbia, with mountains behind his home and the ocean in front. He loved playing outdoors, even in the rain. Every year, he and his nature-loving parents went camping in national parks in Canada and the United States.

When Simon was about seven years old, his parents bought him a camera, and Yellowstone National Park soon became one of his favorite destinations because he loved to photograph the grizzly bears there. It was shortly after a trip to Yellowstone that Simon saw a news report about Kodiak bears needing protection because their forest habitat in Alaska, above the British Columbian border, was being destroyed. These bears reminded Simon of the grizzlies in Yellowstone that he adored.

To help the bears, Simon sent the money he raised from his lemonade stand to the World Wildlife Fund (WWF), a wilderness protection charity. He also sent letters to Canadian Prime Minister Brian Mulroney and United States President George H. W. Bush asking them to help. A short time later, he heard on the news that a sanctuary, or protected area, had been created for the bears. Simon believed it was his letters that had made the difference, although many organizations had, in fact, been involved in protecting the forest. Still, a powerful seed about his role in making change happen had been planted in Simon's mind.

A few years later, at Yellowstone the summer Simon turned thirteen, he met a man who told him about the endangered spirit bears. After hearing about the bears, Simon wanted to help. And he believed other people would want to, too, if only they knew about the plight of these rare bears, which lived roughly six hours away from his home in British Columbia.

But many of the kids Simon's age didn't understand his passion for the bears and nature. In fact, Simon was sometimes bullied for daring to stand up for the things he believed in and just for being different. Eventually, though, Simon's persistence and courage won the respect of his classmates and helped him find like-minded friends.

In 1996, when Simon was fourteen, he shared an ambitious idea with some friends over burgers and chocolate cake in his family's basement. He wanted to create an organization called the Spirit Bear Youth Coalition (SBYC) to raise global awareness about the bears and help ensure their survival. It would have a website with information and resources for members around the world. Simon set to work. He earned the money needed to build the organization by working odd jobs in the community, winning awards with cash prizes at school and selling his handmade gift cards and photography. Roughly four years later, SBYC was so successful that Simon was named one of Sixty Heroes for the Planet by *Time* magazine!

At sixteen, while on a boat trip, Simon met Dr. Jane Goodall, the world-renowned primatologist and conservationist. She overheard him talking about the spirit bears and approached him. They had a picture taken together. About a week later, Simon received the photo in a letter from Dr. Goodall. They traded letters, eventually becoming friends. She was so impressed by Simon that she asked him to work with her at the Jane Goodall Institute, the organization she founded to protect wildlife.

By 2013, the Spirit Bear Youth Coalition had six million members in eighty-five countries and had accomplished what it had set out to do. So Simon closed down SBYC and co-founded CoalitionWILD (www.coalitionwild.org), an organization that provides young people with the tools, resources and mentors they need to create projects that support the causes they believe in.

Simon is still using his voice to inspire others to use theirs and become heroes for the planet. He and his wife, Jill Cooper, live in Calgary, Alberta, where they share stories and photography about the wild world through Ghost Bear Institute (www.ghostbear.org) and run Nature Labs (www.naturelabs.ca), a virtual classroom that provides teaching resources about the wonders of nature and the role of young people in creating a better world for all life.

Spirit Bears

The rare spirit bears are a subspecies (a smaller group within a species) of the North American black bear. They are also known as Kermode bears and by their Indigenous name, *mooksgm'ol*, from the Tsimshian language.

The first spirit bear that Simon Jackson encountered in the Great Bear Rainforest

Most spirit bears are black, and only about one in ten are born with the white fur they are named for. That's because both the mother and father spirit bear must carry the white-fur gene for their young to also be born with white fur. (Genes are passed from parents to offspring and carry the unique plan for the characteristics the babies will inherit, such as their fur color or the shape of their nose.)

Meeting a spirit bear as Simon did was incredibly lucky. Up the Pacific Coast that runs north of Vancouver, British Columbia, there is a group of remote islands now called the Great Bear Rainforest.

Most spirit bears live on just three of these islands: Gribbell, Princess Royal and Pooley Islands. There, some of the trees are so big that it would take you and at least ten of your friends holding hands to circle one. These huge, 10 000-year-old cedar, spruce and other conifer trees provide perfect hiding spots for the spirit bears living there.

It's estimated that there are fewer than a hundred white spirit bears roaming wild and free, and maybe only as few as sixty. No one knows for sure because scientists have a hard time tracking them — they're shy and forage deep inside the densely forested islands.

But thanks to the efforts of the Spirit Bear Youth Coalition, local Indigenous communities, environmentalists and the British Columbia government, the Great Bear Rainforest is now protected from logging (cutting down trees for timber or pulp) and hunting. The spirit bears are at last safe in one of the largest temperate rainforests in the world.

A male spirit bear, roughly fifteen years old, on Princess Royal Island

What You Can Do to Make a Difference

Simon became a champion for the spirit bears and learned how to use his voice to make a difference. Is there something you would like to change to make the world a better place?

Using the power of *your* voice might be something as simple as getting together with some friends and making informational posters to put up around your school. Or you could organize a fundraiser, such as a bake sale or used-book sale, at your school and donate the proceeds to a group doing work you believe in. For inspiration and helpful tips, check out Dr. Jane Goodall's Roots & Shoots program at www.rootsandshoots.org. This organization gives you the opportunity to team up with others working to help the environment, animals or communities, or to start your own mission. Remember, many big changes begin with one voice speaking out.